IMAGES
of America

ETOWAH
COUNTY

IMAGES
of America

ETOWAH
COUNTY

Bob Scarboro and Mike Goodson

ARCADIA
PUBLISHING

ISBN 978-1-5316-1107-1

Published by Arcadia Publishing
Charleston, South Carolina

Library of Congress Catalog Card Number: 98-86142

For all general information contact Arcadia Publishing at:
Telephone 843-853-2070
Fax 843-853-0044
E-Mail sales@arcadiapublishing.com
For customer service and orders:
Toll-Free 1-888-313-2665

Visit us on the Internet at www.arcadiapublishing.com

CONTENTS

ACKNOWLEDGMENTS

Whenever a project such as documenting a county's rich history is undertaken, many factors must be considered. Much history is lost and forgotten each day when cherished photographs are discarded, lost, or destroyed. A great deal of thanks must be shared with the many individuals who have allowed their photos to be copied and preserved in the pages of a publication such as this one. To the many people who have taken time to share a special memory or a precious photograph, the writers of this book are deeply indebted. A special "thank you" is extended to Ann Goodson, who undertook the task of typing the words contained within these pages.

INTRODUCTION

The county we know today as Etowah was created by an act of the state legislature in the year 1866. The county was created from lands from six surrounding counties—Blount, Calhoun, Dekalb, Marshal, St. Clair, and Cherokee.

In November 1866, Alabama's first post-war legislature convened in Montgomery. Senator Augustine L. Woodliff of Cherokee County delivered a petition signed by residents of six counties in hopes of securing the formation of a new county. The bill was easily passed by both the Senate and the House. House Speaker Thomas B. Cooper suggested the name of the county be Baine County in honor of Confederate hero David W. Baine, a former resident of Centre.

Attalla, then known as the Junction, changed its name to Bainsville in an attempt to become the county seat. Gadsden, however, was chosen as the seat of government in a special election. In the election held March 4, 1867, L.E. Hamlin was elected as first probate judge, and Thomas J. Burgess, sheriff. First Baptist Church, located on Broad Street in downtown Gadsden, was used to hold circuit court until the first courthouse could be built.

Baine County only survived one year. When the military government was imposed in 1867, a vote was taken by the Constitutional Convention to abolish the county. On December 1, 1868, the State Legislature repealed the ordinance abolishing the county, and restored the previous boundary lines. County courts were located in Gadsden until a permanent site could be determined in an election scheduled for the following March. The governor was given authority to appoint all county officials. The county name was, however, changed from Baine to Etowah. The name Etowah is a derivative from a Cherokee Indian word "Itawa," which means strong tree.

The story of Etowah County is a story of survival. Etowah County has survived Reconstruction, the Depression, Prohibition, and much turmoil. She has sent her sons into numerous wars and conflicts. The Rainbow Division in World War I proudly marched into battle to defend the freedoms that each Etowah Countian holds so dear.

The history of Etowah County is also a story of her cities and towns. Gadsden, her largest city, was founded in 1846 on the banks of the beautiful Coosa River and was the center of the steamboat trade for the county. The city was originally known as "Double Springs" when it was first settled as a stop on the Huntsville to Rome stage route. Later named Gadsden, in honor of James Gadsden, the city has been the county seat the entire existence of the county.

Attalla, earlier known as the Junction, was settled as a crossroads for the railroad traffic in the area. Known also for a short time as Bainsville, the town has also been known as Newton.

Attalla was the home of the first hydroelectric dam to produce electricity in the state. The dam was built by Captain W.P. Lay, who later founded the Alabama Power Company.

The story of Etowah County is also the story of her smaller cities and towns. Southside, Glencoe, Rainbow City, and Hokes Bluff are rapidly growing and making great contributions to the area. Duck Springs, Reece City, Ridgeville, and Sardis City are towns making an impact on Etowah County—an impact that is positive and necessary for the growth of a county.

The story of Etowah County is also a story of her people. This is a story of the founders of the cities and towns and the people who "grew" the county. This is the story of Daniel C. Turrentine, who was one of the early merchants in the area whose contributions to religion helped many churches in the area grow. This is also about Colonel R.B. Kyle, who helped build a small village into one of the major industrial centers in the state.

The story of Etowah County is also a story of her heroes. The story of Emma Sansom, a 16-year-old girl who helped Confederate General Nathan Bedford Forrest ford Black Creek in his pursuit of Union Colonel Abel Streight. This is also about John W. Wisdom, who rode 67 miles to warn the citizens of Rome, Georgia, about the invading Union army.

The story of Etowah County is also a story of growth. The county has grown in a relatively short time from a sparsely settled area on the stagecoach route through Alabama to a thriving area on the steamboat and railroad routes to an industrial center in the state of Alabama.

The story of this county is also the story of the everyday individuals—the people who work, live in, and contribute to the county's growth each day and the people who make a home such as this one our home.

Many of the photographs contained in these pages were taken by Adolph Lebourg. Born in Normandy, France, in 1887, Adolph Albert Augusta Emmanuel Lebourg immigrated to the United States following the death of his parents. Upon his arrival in the United States, Lebourg traveled south with a carnival. During his travels he learned English and studied basic photography. In 1909, he opened a photography studio in Piper, Alabama. He offered photographic services to patrons in the mining communities of Marvel, Coleanor, Belle Ellen, Savage Creek, Garnsey, and others. The Lebourg photographs are special; their composition and technique reflect exceptional talent. Lebourg took many photographs in the Gadsden area during the 1920s and 1930s. These document many significant events in the history of Etowah County. Lebourg used his love for motorcycles and parades to highlight people in his photographic works.

One

Towns

This is one of the earliest photographs of Broad Street, and it was taken in the fall of 1878. Covered wagons are visible and a well is located at the center of the street. Most of the smaller buildings were destroyed in a spectacular fire on July 4, 1883. The fire was stopped by the fireproof walls of Kyle's Opera House, which is the taller building near the middle of the block. The Opera House itself burned in 1903.

The thriving town of Walnut Grove is shown here in an early photograph from 1884. This small town later would boast of one of the first colleges in Etowah County. The Walnut Grove College was in existence until the late 1890s. The A.S. Nelson Store is pictured on the right.

Construction on one of the many Dwight Mill Village homes is shown in this 1895 photograph. A large village of homes was built to house the many workers that were employed at this Alabama City textile giant until 1958. The homes rented for $4 to $6 per month, depending on the number of rooms.

This is the W.P. Hollingsworth home, located on the northwest corner of Locust Street in 1890. Locust Street, during the early history of Gadsden, had several beautiful homes, although today it is part of Gadsden's downtown business district. This home had a unique ventilation system which provided a form of natural air conditioning.

Crudup is located just north of Reece City near the Dekalb County line. This area of the community was known as Forrest Avenue in this photograph from 1925. This small rural community of Etowah County is located along U.S. Highway 11 and runs parallel to the railroad from Chattanooga to Attalla.

This was the Eliza Klutz home on College Street in Gadsden in 1880. Eliza Klutz is standing just to the left of the large tree. Dr. and Mrs. Sampler are standing to the right of the tree. Dr. Sampler was the first Methodist preacher in Gadsden. The home burned in 1918.

The Kyle home was one of Gadsden's most recognizable homes. This beautiful house was built by Colonel R.B. Kyle in 1888. This residence, later the home of T.S. "Stonewall" Kyle, was torn down during the 1950s to make room for an addition to the present Etowah County Courthouse and a parking lot.

This is the John Wisdom home in Hokes Bluff. Wisdom operated a ferry in the Gadsden area along with Colonel R.B. Kyle. Wisdom gained fame by riding from Gadsden to Rome, Georgia, to warn of the approach of Union Colonel Abel Streight. The city was awakened and prepared, although General Nathan Bedford Forrest overtook Streight before he reached Rome. John Wisdom is known as the "Paul Revere of the South."

This is the Moragne home, located at 606 South Fourth Street. This is a fine example of one of the early homes located in the Gadsden area. Many beautiful homes were found throughout the downtown Gadsden area. A good many of these homes have been destroyed to make room for businesses.

The Bellinger home was another of Gadsden's beautiful houses. The home was located on the southwest corner of Twelfth Street and Chestnut Street, the present site of the Gadsden Board of Education annex building.

This is downtown Attalla looking east toward Gadsden. Attalla was known as "the Junction" because several railroads intersected at this point. The Gadsden, Attalla, and Alabama City Railroad tracks and overhead wires are seen in this photograph. Note that the streets are unpaved.

This is an aerial view of the Coosa River, which flows through Etowah County. This 1930 photograph shows the L & N Railroad trestle, which was the first bridge across the river and was built in the late 1880s. The Memorial Bridge, which was built in 1927 to commemorate the Rainbow Division in World War I, united Gadsden with East Gadsden.

This was the old covered bridge in Duck Springs during the 1940s. Covered bridges similar to this one at one time were found throughout the Etowah County area. This bridge was destroyed by vandals over the years.

This photograph shows the 31st anniversary of J.C. Penney's store, located at this time on the corner of Broad and Third Streets. Notice the sidewalk scales outside the store. A person could get their weight and fortune for one penny. The Etowah County Courthouse is located in the background of this 1932 photo.

"Hoovertowns," much like this one, were scattered throughout the country during the Great Depression. This shantytown was located on the banks of Black Creek near Tuscaloosa Avenue in Gadsden. The houses were made of scrap lumber, packing crates, and anything that could protect the occupants from the cold and rain. Hoovertowns became nonexistent following World War II and the booming post-war economy.

This shows Gadsden's Broad Street looking east in 1940 from Seventh Street. The clock tower of the Etowah County Courthouse is in the center of the photograph. The white dome of Gadsden's City Hall is on the left. The Pitman Theatre would later occupy the property next to the Texaco Station on the left.

This is the old cannon overlooking the Coosa River. The cannon stood between Broad Street and Locust Street in Gadsden looking out over the Coosa River. This 1930s photograph shows the cannon before it was scrapped during World War II. This "landmark" was sold for scrap metal during one of the many metal drives during the World War II.

This is Broad Street looking east in 1950. Snellgrove's Drug Store is located on the corner. Snellgrove's was a landmark on Broad Street from 1930 to 1993. The Saul's Hotel is across the street. This is the main business district in downtown Gadsden. Note the parking in one block is diagonal and parallel in the other.

Downtown Attalla's business district is shown here on a busy day in 1950. People from Walnut Grove, Gallant, Keener, Reece City, and Ivalee would come to Etowah County's second-largest city to shop and transact day-to-day business. Attalla offered a variety of stores, banks, and two movie theaters over the years.

This photograph shows the demolition of the second Etowah County Courthouse. A wrecking ball was used to knock down the brick walls of the structure. The property was sold by the County after much controversy, and a new W.T. Grant Store was built on the site. Railroad Furniture occupies the property today.

Alabama City is seen here in this photograph taken in early 1960. The Dwight Manufacturing Company is shown at the heart of this former industrial city. Alabama City was founded to lure industry to the Gadsden and Attalla areas. "Wall Street," the business district of this small town, is shown in the lower left. The town later merged with Gadsden, and the mill was torn down.

This 1950 aerial view shows downtown Attalla's main business district. Attalla is Etowah County's second largest town, and has also been known as the "Junction," because of the

location of the railroads in the area. Because of the importance of these railroads to Etowah County, Attalla was considered for the county seat on two occasions.

Noccalula Falls is located atop Lookout Mountain in Gadsden. The falls, originally known as Black Creek Falls, is one of Etowah County's most beautiful scenic attractions. The name was later changed to Noccalula Falls after a Native American princess who jumped to her death at the falls. Legend has it that Noccalula wanted to marry a brave from her own tribe. Noccalula's father, the tribal chieftain, had arranged for her marriage to a brave from a neighboring tribe. Rather than marry someone she did not love, Noccalula jumped to her death into the gorge below. Native American writings found on stones below the falls confirmed the legend. The falls has long been a tourist attraction. A streetcar line was built to the falls to transport tourists from the riverboat landing downtown.

Two

BUSINESSES

The Isom and Ralls Hospital was located on Sixth Avenue in 1905. The hospital burned and was quickly rebuilt by Dr. A.W. Ralls. The hospital was later organized under the name Forrest General Hospital in 1928 and was later sold to the Etowah Baptist Association.

The Printup Hotel was one of Gadsden's most beautiful early hotels. The hotel is located on the corner of Fourth and Locust Streets in downtown Gadsden. The hotel was managed by Adolph Reich during its years of operation as a hotel. The structure was ravaged by two destructive fires: the first fire in 1910 and another in 1928.

This is the main lobby of Gadsden's Printup Hotel in 1900. This beautiful four-story hotel experienced two major fires during its years of operation. The lobby has a movie poster advertising an attraction at Gadsden's Imperial Theatre. The building is still standing, although it has gone through several changes following these fires.

Gadsden's Mineral Springs Hotel is shown here in a late 1912 photograph. The hotel, originally known as the Bellevue Hotel, was built on the brow of Lookout Mountain, overlooking Gadsden, at a cost of $35,000. The beautiful structure was built in 1889 by the Gadsden Land and Improvement Company. The hotel was converted into the Jones Female College in 1895 and was attended by students from several states. Louie Hart purchased the hotel in 1910 and reorganized the property into the Mineral Springs Hotel, which contained 72 rooms, a spacious ballroom, a large dining hall, and several parlors. The grand hotel was destroyed on June 5, 1912, in a spectacular fire that could be seen throughout Etowah County. The cause of the fire was listed as wiring, although a possible lightning strike could not be ruled out.

These are the ruins of the Mineral Springs Hotel after the spectacular fire of June 5, 1912. The tragic fire was listed as electrical wiring, although Gadsden had experienced a thunderstorm earlier and some speculation was given to a lightning strike. This is an early Lebourg photograph from 1914 showing the rock foundation of the beautiful structure.

Gadsden's first hospital was established in 1905 by Drs. C.L. Guice and George W. Faucett, and was known as the Guice and Faucett Infirmary. It was located in the two-story residence of W.H. Denson on Forrest Avenue. This hospital burned a short time later. After the fire, Dr. Guice leased the Slack residence on Chestnut Street and continued to run his infirmary for some time.

Clyburn and Padden Millinery Company was located at Canterberry Station in Alabama City. Canterberry Station was one of the business districts in Alabama City, located between Gadsden and Attalla. The people in this 1915 photograph from left to right are as follows: Dozier Gibbs, Jake Flynt, Jack L. Martin, Maude Roberts, Walter Hunt, Octavia Clyburn, Alma Skeen Bailey, Myrtle Skeen Glazner, Earl Skeen, Ruth Graham Burkolzer, Lily Skeen Goode, Fulton "Foots" Skeen, Lillie Cambron, Amelia Brown Foster, Loda Morgan, and Loda Padden.

This was one of the more famous spots in Gadsden's red light district in 1905. Saloons were found in the downtown area, with many located on Broad Street. This was Motlow's Saloon in the 400 block of Broad Street. Spoon Motlow operated a saloon as well as a distillery in Gadsden. When Etowah County was voted dry in 1907, Motlow moved his operation to Tennessee. This is now the famous Jack Daniel's Distillery.

The J.M. Adams Store was an important facet of life in the Keener area. This is a photograph from 1910 showing the Keener community in Etowah County. Keener is located just north of Reece City, near the Etowah-Dekalb County line on U.S. Highway 11.

The Attalla Furniture Company is shown here on a busy day in 1912. People from the small communities of Keener, Reece City, Gallant, Ivalee, and Sardis would make the trip to town on Saturdays to shop in the different stores. Stalks of bananas are hanging on the front of the store in this picture. The streets were unpaved, and the streetcar tracks and overhead wires can be seen.

This 1920 photograph shows the beautiful Dwight Inn in Alabama City. The hotel was located on Dwight Square, near the entrance to Dwight Manufacturing Company, a giant textile mill built in 1895. The inn, or "boardinghouse" as it was called, was the home of many visiting company executives. The hotel was destroyed in a spectacular fire in 1927. Many curious onlookers watched in a cold rain as Alabama City's only hotel burned to the ground.

28

This 1925 photograph shows the First State Bank of Altoona. Altoona is located northwest of Attalla near the Blount County line. Pictured here at the bank are, from left to right, T.R. Bynum, Coy Shelton, Clarence Hardin, Johnny Spicer, and Jim Reed. The bank is still in operation.

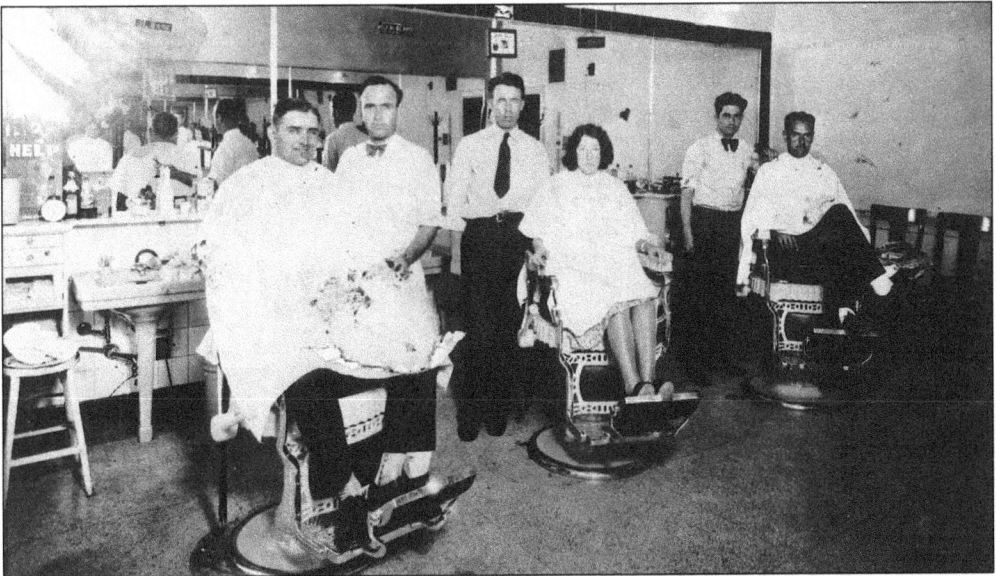

This is the barbershop located in Gadsden's beautiful Reich Hotel. The hotel was owned by Adolph Reich and a group of investors. Several shops were located in the hotel, including the barbershop. The barbers standing are, from left to right, as follows: J.L. Ware, J.H. Beard, and B. Woodham.

Gadsden's first skyscraper was the ten-story Reich Hotel. The hotel was built in 1929 by a group of investors headed by A.P. Reich. The hotel was built at a time when Gadsden was experiencing rapid growth. Adolph Reich also owned the Printup Hotel, Gadsden's other downtown hotel. The Reich Hotel was in operation for 50 years with Gadsden resident Vera Springfield working there for the entire time.

This was an early gas station in Alabama City. This station was located on Elliott Avenue, next to the Elliott Grammar School on what is now Meighan Boulevard. The avenue, as well as the school, was named for Captain James M. Elliott Jr., one of the founders of Alabama City. This building is still standing and looks much as it did in this early photograph.

Snellgrove's Drug Store was a downtown landmark for 63 years. This 1930 photograph shows the interior of one of Gadsden's oldest drugstores. Pictured from left to right are as follows: Max Moseley, Inzer Ferrell, T.C. McCollum, A.J. Pressley, Austin Ferrell, and Howard West. Max Moseley purchased the store in 1963 and continued to operate the business until it closed in 1993.

The Holy Name of Jesus Hospital is shown here on its dedication. The groundbreaking for this hospital was July 2, 1930. The hospital is located on First Street near Moragne Park, on the banks of the Coosa River. The hospital, with later additions, is now called Riverview Medical Center.

Gadsden's General Hospital is shown here in a 1925 photograph. This hospital was built in 1917 by Dr. J.E. Leach on Chestnut Street between Fifth and Sixth Streets. The structure is now part of the seven-story Noojin Building. The buildings are located next to the First Presbyterian Church.

The Forrest Hotel was a downtown hotel located on Chestnut Street, near the present site of the Daughette Towers. The hotel served as both a hotel and boardinghouse. This hotel was later torn down after the construction of Gadsden's first skyscraper, the Reich Hotel.

This is a group of men sitting around out front of the J.W. Moody Store at Canoe Creek, near Rainbow City, in 1930. A group such as this was usually found hanging around discussing everything from politics and weather to Alabama and Auburn football.

Neighborhood stores such as the Noccalula Cash Store were important during the early days of Etowah County. A person could pick up essential items at one of these small stores without having to make the long trip to downtown Gadsden or Attalla. This store, located on the mountain near Noccalula Falls, was owned and operated by W.F. Ramsey.

This is the A.S. Norton Store, located in Attalla. Dry good stores such as this one were found throughout Etowah County at the turn of the twentieth century. A.J. Norton is pictured at the left, with Carrie Belle Norton on the right.

Hansard's was located in the right front corner of the Princess Theatre. Before the days of theater concession stands, Hansard's sold popcorn and peanuts to movie patrons. Hansard's will long be remembered as having the best hot dogs in the Gadsden area. Later, Hansard's moved across the street next to the Capitol Theatre. This 1938 picture shows a sign advertising cigarettes for 15¢ a pack.

This was Gadsden's Terminal Hotel in 1940. The hotel was originally the W.P. Lay home on Forrest Avenue. The building was moved back to First Avenue, near the L & N Railroad, and converted to a hotel. W.P. Lay, the founder of the Alabama Power Company, built a new home, which is visible in the background. The Lay home was on the present site of the Alabama Power Company. The steps at the left are all that remains of the hotel and the railroad terminal.

William Boykin Day is shown here behind the counter at his store in Alabama City. The store was in operation in the 1940s. A person could pick up anything they needed at a neighborhood grocery store such as this. With the coming of the large chain stores, neighborhood stores such as this have faded into our past and taken a place in history.

Dooly Grill was a favorite hangout during the 1950s for students from Emma Sansom High School. The grill, located at 3232 Forrest Avenue, was owned and operated by Burnis A. and Nettie L. Dooly. The grill offered curb service, like many other eating establishments of the day. Wrenn's Ice Cream, a local favorite, was also advertised.

Etowah County's Tuberculosis Hospital is seen here in this 1962 photograph. The new hospital is shown in the foreground, with the old structure located in the upper left. Interstate 59, then under construction, is visible in the background. The building now houses Mountainview Hospital.

Woody's Grocery was located in Ivalee, Alabama, just west of Attalla. This 1945 photograph shows the interior of the store that was so important to this small community. It would save a person a long trip to Attalla or an even longer one to Gadsden if they could pick up what they needed here.

Arthur Green is shown here in front of his place of business. Arthur Green's Barber Shop was located on North Fourth Street for many years. The shop later moved to Broad Street when several of these buildings were torn down to make room for a parking lot. Arthur Green will long be remembered for his contributions to his community and city.

This 1949 photo shows Neely's Store, located at Peachtree and Eleventh Streets in Gadsden. This was a great example of a local grocery store. A store such as this was located every three or four blocks in each neighborhood. Most of these little home-owned and operated stores did business on credit.

This was Crossfield's Ice Cream Parlor, located on Forrest Avenue in Gadsden. Crossfield's made ice cream and also ran an ice plant. The trucks from the ice plant would drive through the neighborhoods clanging a bell for customers to come out and buy ice for their iceboxes. This photograph is from the early 1950s.

This is the Baptist Memorial Hospital, under construction in 1958. The new structure was built in East Gadsden, near the Goodyear Tire and Rubber Company. This new facility replaced the old hospital located near Gadsden High School in West Gadsden. The hospital was later sold and is now the Gadsden Regional Medical Center.

Three

PASTIMES

Elliott Park Lake was a popular amusement park during the early 1900s. The park was frequented by residents of Alabama City, Attalla, and Gadsden who would spend a Sunday afternoon watching a ballgame or enjoying a boat ride on the lake. The park had a lake, bandstand, baseball park, skating rink, and outdoor theater. The park was later known as the Masonic Lake.

This 1907 photograph shows the Duck Springs Odd Fellows. W.A. Simpson was the grand master and is pictured on the front row, fourth from the right. Arthur C. Guest is on the third row, second from left. T.A. "Bud" Guest is also on the third row, first from the right. This photograph is courtesy of Eddie Guest.

The Zamora Shrine Temple Band is shown here marching on a July 4th parade on Broad Street in downtown Gadsden. The Etowah County Courthouse is in the background. The sign on the front of the courthouse says, "Here July 4th Daredevil Vickery." Lowell Vickery dove from the clock tower into a tank of water. Vickery had earlier gained fame when he dove from Noccalula Falls and lived to tell about it. He later announced he would dive from the L & N railroad trestle into the Coosa River, although local authorities prevented this feat.

42

An Armistice Day celebration is shown here in downtown Gadsden. When the end of World War I was announced, the entire town took a holiday. A parade took place through downtown Gadsden, followed by fireworks and a band concert. The "war to end all wars" had come to an end, and the world was again at peace.

Gadsden's Belle Theatre was located on Broad Street from 1912 until the early 1930s. The theater, owned by Mr. and Mrs. W.B. Woods, advertised the finest "photoplays" around. Mom and Pop Woods owned Wood's Cut Rate Grocery, which was also located on Broad Street. The Belle Theatre was one of Gadsden's more popular early theaters.

Gadsden's beautiful Hayden-Pake Theatre was opened in 1908. The theater, later renovated and renamed the Gadsden Theatre, was the home of many live shows, vaudeville, and the finest in motion pictures. "Boob" Brasfield was a local favorite who appeared on the stage regularly. The theater closed in the late 1950s and was torn down to make room for the drive-in tellers of the American National Bank.

This late-1800s photograph shows an art class that was being taught in the Gadsden area. Music and art were enjoyed throughout the Etowah County area, with many prominent citizens participating in classes such as this one.

This 1915 photograph shows Adolph Lebourg seated on one of his Indian motorcycles. Lebourg was fascinated with motorcycles and photography. During his years in the Gadsden area, Lebourg captured much of Etowah County's history through both still and motion pictures. Lebourg operated a sporting goods store on Broad Street and also repaired radios. Lebourg was killed in a boating accident on Lake Guntersville on Easter Sunday, 1958.

The "Whole Gadsden Bunch" is shown in a 1912 photograph from the Adolph Lebourg collection. This was a group of motorcycle enthusiasts who rode Indian motorcycles. Shown from left to right are as follows: Joe Lumpkin, Adolph Lebourg, Fred Pruitt, Ernest Phillips, Audie King, Bill Sexton, and G.E. Gay. The "Gadsden Bunch" participated in many endurance races and were seen everywhere on their Indians.

On September 6, 1926, a high-tension wire was struck by lightning and fell to the ground into a crowd of people who had gathered to watch a circus parade. Two people in the crowd were killed and five were injured when the wire fell. T.E. Bowling and Imogene Isaacs, both of Alabama City, were pronounced dead at the scene. Fifteen horses belonging to the Christy Brothers Circus were also killed when the 22,000-volt wire burned and fell to the ground. The wires ran from the steam plant to the streetcar barn and to Attalla. The mishap took place as the circus parade was forming near the present site of Emma Sansom High School in Alabama City.

Alabama City's Palace Theatre was located on Seventh Street, or "Wall Street," during the 1920s. The theater was owned and operated by William Broom, who operated several movie houses over the years in Alabama City. Johnny Bolin ran the movie projector, and Winter Shropshire played the piano. Broom would drive around Alabama City in an old pickup truck covered with movie posters to advertise the movies. He was accompanied by a monkey and a tame bear on these drives. This theater was later named the Marcelle Theatre. This photograph is courtesy of Mrs. Monroe Smith.

Gadsden's Princess Theatre is shown here in a 1933 photograph. The Princess Theatre, originally known as the Imperial, was one of Gadsden's most successful theaters. The theater's manager, D.B. Dixon, was known for his many great promotions. The Princess was on the corner of Broad and Fifth Streets, the present site of the Center for Cultural Arts.

Gadsden's "new" Princess Theatre is shown here at night. The Princess was remodeled in 1937 into one of the most beautiful small-town theaters in this part of the country. The Art Deco exterior, along with a completely refurbished interior, transformed the Princess into a showplace. Manager D.B. Dixon was a master promoter for this theater.

The Gadsden Country Club swimming pool was known for its extremely cold water. The pool was fed by an underground spring and the water was always unusually cold. Pool patrons are seen here in a photograph from 1930. The Country Club is located on the former site of the Elliott Peach Orchard.

The Gadsden Country Club is shown here in a 1960 photograph. The new Country Club facility is shown on the left, with the original club on the right just before its destruction. The club was organized on July 25, 1919, when a group of businessmen met and elected Otto Agricola the first president. The club was incorporated August 20, 1919, with 250 share-holding members, each putting up $1,000 for a share of stock.

Bicycle races were popular in the early 1900s in the Etowah County area. This 1914 Lebourg photograph shows one such race through the streets of Gadsden. Many curious spectators were gathered on both sides of the street to watch this race. Match races were held at Elliott Lake Park.

Dwight Park was the scene of many great sporting events in the early days of Alabama City. The "Dwights," an outstanding baseball team, are shown here playing a game at the park in 1920. Dwight Park was also the home of many great football games, as well as other special events. The park was located near Black Creek.

50

During the days of the Great Depression, children in the Etowah County area had to make their own toys. These makeshift cars were made from wood crudely cut and put together with nails and wire. The wheels were cut from logs, and holes were burned into them with hot pokers.

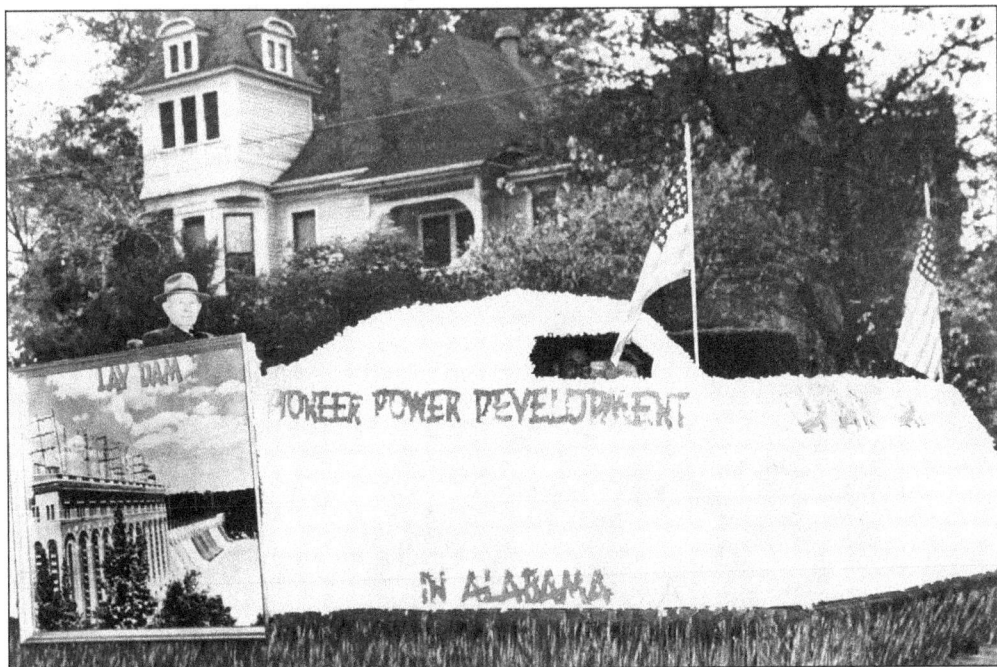

Captain W.P. Lay is shown here riding in a Gadsden parade during the 1940s. William Patrick Lay is known as the founder of the Alabama Power Company. The Lay home is seen in the background on Forrest Avenue in downtown Gadsden. This is the present site of the Gadsden Office of the Alabama Power Company.

Everyone loves a good parade. Parades have always stirred a lot of interest in the Etowah County area, from Christmas parades to the local high school homecoming parades. This float from a 1940 parade is from Crossfield's Ice Cream Parlor. Crossfield's operated an icehouse and also one of the most popular ice cream parlors of the 1950s.

The band from Camp Sibert leads a parade down Broad Street in Gadsden. This was a World War II war bond parade from 1944. A B-25 did a fly-over during the parade. This photograph was made looking east, with the old U.S. Post Office on the right.

The Gadsden Pilots were a Class B ball club playing in the Southeastern League during the 1946 season. The Pilots are shown here in a game at city park, the present site of the City Sports Complex on Meighan Boulevard. The Pilots were paced during the 1946 season by local favorite Byron "Barney" Bridgers. The ball club was well promoted, and the games were well attended. Lee Blaine was the voice of the Pilots, and Byron Todd was the club's president during its first year of operation. J.C. Oakes won a 1947 Hudson during one of the many promotions at a home game.

The Gadsden Municipal Pool was the site of many swim meets. This 1946 photograph shows one such meet between Gadsden and Anniston. Gadsden's Convention Hall is located in the background. This swimming pool, like several others around the county, has been closed, and most have been filled in.

This is a Gadsden High School homecoming parade from 1949. This photo was made in front of Pollock Motor Company, and the bus station is visible if one looks west. Homecoming parades are eagerly awaited each year. Gadsden, Litchfield, and Emma Sansom High have their parades in downtown Gadsden each year.

This 1956 photograph shows an Emma Sansom "Rebel" homecoming parade. This photo was made on Fifth and Broad Streets, with Gadsden's beautiful Princess Theatre on the corner. The Kyle building is shown with the Top Value Stamps advertisement on the side. The Kyle building is currently being restored to become part of the Center for Cultural Arts.

54

The Bama Theatre was located on Forrest Avenue in Alabama City during the 1950s. The Bama opened during the years following World War II, when many movie houses opened in the Etowah County area. The Bama was a favorite place to spend a Saturday afternoon watching a good western. This building later housed a skating rink. This photo is courtesy of Jack McGill.

Sergeant Ola Mize is shown here in a parade in downtown Gadsden. Sergeant Mize was awarded the Congressional Medal of Honor for his acts of heroism on the field of battle during the Korean Conflict. Mize was credited with saving the lives of many of his troops during a 14-hour battle in June 1953. The event took place on Outpost Harry in South Korea. During the engagement, Mize killed approximately 65 of the enemy.

Lake Rhea was one of Etowah County's favorite amusement attractions. The lake grew to be a landmark after it was purchased by Mr. and Mrs. Charles Murphy in 1948. Under the ownership of the Murphy family, the lake expanded to contain a dance pavilion, picnic area, rides, and carpet golf, as well as a giant spring-fed swimming pool. The Murphys sold the lake to the City of Attalla in 1978.

Each year, Gadsden's Municipal Airport would host an air show, which was sponsored by the Civil Air Patrol. This photograph from 1959 shows one such show. The large hanger was built during World War II, when the airport was part of Camp Sibert. The City took control of the airport in 1947 when the army installation was closed.

Duncan Renaldo, otherwise known as the Cisco Kid, made an appearance in the Gadsden area in 1964. During the 1950s and early 1960s, several "movie stars" made appearances in the Etowah County area to promote movies that were playing at the local movie theaters. A large crowd is shown here watching "Cisco" perform.

Saturdays were always spent at the kiddie matinee at Gadsden's beautiful Pitman Theatre. The kiddie shows were popular during the 1960s, when a movie-goer could spend a Saturday morning at the show for six R.C. Cola bottle caps. The Pitman was opened September 26, 1947, with the movie *Slavegirl* as the premiere attraction. One of Gadsden's most popular theaters, the Pitman, closed in 1981. This photograph is courtesy of Jack Sherer.

Four

INDUSTRIES

The Alabama Furnace Company is shown here in this 1880 photograph. The furnace was one of the many industries owned and operated by Colonel Robert B. Kyle. Colonel Kyle owned several businesses throughout Etowah County and, at one time, owned over 300 houses in the Gadsden–Alabama City area. The Alabama Furnace Company was located on the banks of the Coosa River in North Gadsden and was one of the largest coke furnaces in the South.

The Consolidated Coal and Iron Company was built in 1887–1888. The iron company had a capacity to produce 125 tons a day. The name of the company was later changed to Sloss-Sheffield.

Gadsden and Attalla has had several pipe shops over the years. This was the Coosa Pipe and Foundry Company, located in north Gadsden, on the banks of the Coosa River. Foundries such as this one employed many Etowah County residents.

Many mines were located in the foothills throughout Etowah County. This mine, located at Reece City during the 1890s, employed a large workforce of Etowah County citizens. Several mines were located in the Reece City and Keener areas. Hours were long and the work was hard and dangerous. Working conditions at best were primitive, as shown in this photo.

This 1910 photograph shows a conveyor that was used to pull logs out of the Coosa River at one of the sawmills in Gadsden. Logs were floated down river from Ball Play or brought upriver from the Greensport area. The logs were tied together with hickory bark, pegs, and saplings.

This is a group of laborers from the Elliott Peach Orchard. The Elliott Peach Orchard grew and canned peaches that were shipped all over the world. The orchard was located at the present site of the Gadsden Country Club and golf course. This 1906 photograph shows a lot of children who were used in the picking and canning of the peaches.

Marshal Pence is shown with a team of oxen hauling logs in the Ball Play area of Etowah County. A lot of timber was cut in this area and hauled to the Coosa River and floated to one of the sawmills in Gadsden. Families living in this area included the Wagnons, Pollards, Tumlins, Woods, and Freeman families. This photo is from 1921.

The Etowah Cotton Warehouse is shown in this 1920 photograph. Bales and bales of cotton are also shown here around the warehouse. Farmers would bring their wagons loaded with cotton to the warehouse, then park and sleep under the wagon while waiting to have them unloaded. The Etowah County Jail is shown in the background.

This photograph from the 1920s shows one of the many cotton fields throughout the Etowah County area. A large labor force was needed to pick the cotton each year. A good many older people and children were used to harvest the crops around the turn of the century, as this photograph would indicate.

Braswell's Mill was located near Walnut Grove in western Etowah County. Mills such as this one were important to local residents during the early 1940s. Shown in this photograph are, from left to right, Mr. and Mrs. John Hopper and Mr. and Mrs. George Cole.

This is Pollard's Gin, located in the Ball Play area of Etowah County, in 1928. Several cotton gins were located throughout the county during the early part of the twentieth century. The Pollard family was one of the more prominent families in the Ball Play area.

This is William Patrick Lay's first hydroelectric dam on Big Wills Creek near Attalla. The dam was built over a four-year period beginning in 1899. This plant transmitted the state's first electric current some 5 miles through wire attached to insulators nailed to trees to light the city of Attalla. Lay was known as the father of the Alabama Power Company and was its first president.

This is the Owen's Syrup Mill in the fall of 1915. The mill was located at the Owens Farm in South Gadsden. The family produced 2,000 gallons of syrup one fall and sold it for $1 a gallon. The dark syrup sold for 50¢ a gallon. The dark syrup was dark because the cane was grown on dark, creek-bottom land.

This is M.C. Taylor's first steam shovel. The shovel is shown here making the first cut in the Littleton Road. Taylor Construction Company cut the road to Littleton in 1924. Littleton is located near Attalla in northern Etowah County.

The Dwight Mill, located in Alabama City, is shown here in this 1930 photograph. Pictured here is the site before later additions were made to the textile giant, which grew to be one of the largest in the United States. The mill was the center of life in the town of Alabama City. The mill closed in 1958 and was torn down in the late 1970s.

The smoldering embers of the Gadsden Car Works are all that remains of one of Etowah County's larger employers of the early 1900s. The industry was founded as the Elliott Car Works in 1888 and employed 300 people at the height of production. The car works produced boxcars and all types of railroad cars. Captain Elliott sold the car works following a labor dispute. It was after one of these labor disputes that the car works burned in 1923.

Excitement was the order of the day when the Goodyear Blimp visited the Etowah County area. This 1934 photograph shows the airship *Vigilant* landing near the Gadsden plant. A large hanger for the blimp was located behind the giant tire and rubber manufacturing plant. Doug Phillips was killed while helping to land the blimp on a windy day. A large group of men would catch lines to land the blimp. The ship started back up and everyone turned loose except Phillips. The pilot attempted to reach the river, but Phillips fell off before reaching the water.

The Goodyear plant's first load of tires is shown being shipped out in mid-1929. The tire manufacturer was built in a four-and-one-half month period of that year. The driver of this first load was Fred Locklear, and the owner of the freight line was Pete Barnett.

Goodyear's giant tire manufacturing plant in East Gadsden is one of Etowah County's largest employers. The plant was built in early 1929. Ground was broken in February, and the first tire rolled off the assembly line on June 21st. Over 20,000 were on hand for the formal dedication on July 11, 1929.

Glencoe has been the home of at least five rock quarries over the years. This is the quarry of LaGarde Lime and Stone Company, located on Highway 431 near the Etowah-Calhoun County line. The quarries were Glencoe's largest employers during the early part of the twentieth century.

Clayton's Mill was located in Alabama City. Water from the mill pond was piped to Dwight Manufacturing Company a few miles away. Dwight Manufacturing Company was one of the largest cotton mills in the United States at this time. The mill shown here in this 1920 photo later burned, and all that remains is the mill pond.

This 1930 photograph shows the Gadsden Curb Market. The market was located on South Eighth Street, where the Etowah Health Department is today. The curb market was on the Elliott property—note the large walnut tree growing through the roof.

Employees of Gadsden's Republic Steel Corporation are shown here during the first strike at the Gadsden plant. A large group of employees are seen here at the main entrance to the plant. The Gulfsteel YMCA is shown at the left, and an ice truck is pictured in the foreground. Trucks such as this delivered ice to residents in the area.

This beautiful building near the entrance to the Republic Steel Corporation was originally built as an employee's clubhouse. This 1918 photograph shows the structure shortly after completion. This was later the Gulfsteel YMCA. For years, the YMCA was the place to go in Alabama City. The building housed a gymnasium, pool, game room, and even showed motion pictures during the 1920s. The building is no longer standing.

This was Silver Dollar Day in Etowah County. Gulf States Steel would make their payroll in silver dollars to impress the community as to how the money moved through the city. The truck on the left is a RKO news truck making a newsreel to show at the theaters.

Republic Steel Corporation's Gulfsteel Division is located in Gadsden. The steel maker has been one of Etowah County's largest employers from its early beginnings. The mill was built in 1902 as the Alabama Steel and Wire Company. The company was reorganized in 1906 as the Southern Steel Company. In 1913, it changed ownership and was operated for 25 years as the Gulf States Steel Company.

Gadsden's economy received an encouraging lift in 1902 when the Alabama Steel and Wire Company of Birmingham built a plant on land donated by a group of citizens. William Patrick Lay, the founder of the Alabama Power Company, spearheaded the campaign. This is the interior of the wire mill in 1925.

This is the Price Ice Company on First Avenue in 1955. Several icehouses were found throughout the Etowah County area. Ice was sold in large blocks, as well as being crushed at these icehouses. The icehouse became a thing of the past with the coming of freezers and refrigerators.

This is an interior view of the Price Ice House. Note the large blocks of ice that were sold by the pound.

Five

CIVIL SERVICE

This is an artist's rendering of Etowah County's original courthouse. The drawing was done by Danny Crownover from a description in the county commission minutes. The courthouse was built in 1870 on property near Fourth and Broad Streets in downtown Gadsden at a cost of $12,990. Colonel R.B. Kyle and W.P. Lay paid the cost of the construction.

This was Etowah County's second courthouse. This structure was dedicated on October 25, 1890, and was built at a cost of $70,000. The building was a brick structure trimmed in blue granite. The most impressive feature of the courthouse was the 126-foot-high clock tower. The building was easily accessible by two winding stairways in the front and one at the rear. A small park was located at the rear, complete with a fountain and overhanging trees, making it an ideal place to relax and visit. This photograph was taken in 1910, before the streets were paved in downtown Gadsden.

This was Etowah County's second courthouse in 1949. The square block at the base of the clock tower was originally used as a step to enter or exit a buggy or wagon. After automobiles replaced buggies, the step was moved back from the street and was used by preachers preaching in front of the courthouse. This photograph shows the renovations to the structure—a third floor had been added, a portico had been added to the front, and the clock tower had been blocked.

This photograph shows the present Etowah County Courthouse. This structure was built to replace the old courthouse on Broad Street. The courthouse occupies the property that once was the site of the Kyle and Elliott homes. This 1964 photo shows the county's government complex site on Forrest Avenue in Gadsden.

Here, construction is underway on the U.S. Post Office on Broad Street in downtown Gadsden. The construction took place during 1912. The post office was located on the corner of Sixth and Broad Streets. The building currently houses federal government offices. The post office was originally a one-story building.

The U.S. Post Office is shown here in a 1920 photograph, after the addition of the second floor. In the left background is the Episcopal church, which was located at this time at the corner of Sixth and Chestnut Streets.

The U.S. Post Office in Gadsden was undergoing an addition in 1936. This building housed the post office until it was heavily damaged in a fire. The structure was renovated and now houses many of the federal agencies in the Etowah County area.

The Gadsden Police Department is shown here in an 1885 photograph. From left to right are the following: (seated) Bill Thornton, Chief Henry C. White, and Emmett Wheeler; (standing) Will Thomas, Sam O'Bannon, Jim Singleton, and Bob Leath. Sam O'Bannon later served as the police chief when Etowah County was voted dry in 1907 and the saloons on Broad Street were closed.

This was the Gadsden Police Department in the year 1912. Shown from left to right are the following: Chief Bowers, John Cunningham, Nick Littlefield, John Roberson, Ross Bates, Morris Roper, "Bad Eye" Strickland, Bill Allen, Will Thornton, and Harvey Elliott (seated on the motorcycle). This photograph was taken in front of City Hall.

Sheriff Bob Leath and deputies are shown inspecting a moonshine still in the Ball Play area of Etowah County. Moonshining was widespread throughout the county during Prohibition. A large quantity of illegal alcohol is shown in this 1935 photograph. Ball Play is located between Hokes Bluff and the Cherokee County line.

This is the old Etowah County Jail. The jail was located on North Third Street, near Meighan Boulevard. The jail was being torn down in this photograph and was moved when the present Etowah County Courthouse was built in 1950.

Here, Etowah County sheriff's deputies are disposing of illegal contraband alcohol. Moonshine and illegal liquor sales were a problem in the days when Etowah County was "dry." Etowah County was voted "wet" in the early 1970s. This alcohol was poured into the gutters and the containers were smashed at the front of the Etowah County Courthouse on Forrest Avenue.

Members of the Gadsden Police Department are shown in a photograph taken outside of the Police Building at Gadsden's new City Hall. Police Chief Charles Cary had an outstanding department, and Gadsden has always had a low crime rate. Cary was chief during the early 1970s.

Members of the Gadsden Police Department are pictured here in a photograph taken May 3, 1936, on the front steps of the Gadsden City Hall, located on North Fifth Street. The crime rate during the days of the Depression was low, and the Gadsden Police Department was to be commended.

These are the city officials of Alabama City in 1913. From left to right are the following: (seated) Police Chief Joe Williams, Walter Washam, Jim Hill, J.H. "Jimmy" Snyder, and George Thacker; (standing) Mayor Burns, city council members Henry Williams, J.D. Loner, Tom Cox, Ira Gray, and Tom Barron, and City Clerk Charley West.

Attalla's first fire engine was the first fire engine in Etowah County. Shown on the truck from left to right are John Bigham, Joe Ramey, Luke Woods, John Holgam, and Johnny Chergotakis.

These are the city of Attalla's finest in 1951. This photograph shows the town's city employees standing in front of one of the city's firetrucks. From left to right are the following: (front row) Irving Smith (police), Ralph Burgess (city council), C.C. Yother (fireman [paid]), Jack Jones (volunteer), John Bigham (assistant chief), Mrs. Catherine Burke, Tommy Hinton (volunteer), R.V. Smith (fireman [paid]), John Holgan (fire chief), Edmond Sheeley (volunteer), and Sidney Hinton (volunteer); (back row) J.D. Smith Sr. (city council), Herbert Phillips (volunteer), Jack Smith (volunteer), Eugene Gray (volunteer), and Tom Carnes (volunteer).

Firefighters are shown fighting a fire at the Woodliff Furniture Company. The store was located on the corner of Fifth and Broad Streets in downtown Gadsden. A large crowd of onlookers is also shown in this 1910 photograph.

This turn-of-the-century photograph shows Gadsden's early horse-drawn fire engines. The steam engine at the right had replaced a hand-pumper the City had purchased in November of 1882. Captain James M. Elliott Jr. was the first fire chief. This photo was taken in front of Gadsden's City Hall.

Gadsden's fire engines are shown outside City Hall in this 1925 photograph. The Central Fire Station was located in the City Hall Building on North Fifth Street. City Hall was later moved to a new structure at the corner of First Street and Chestnut Street. A new Central Fire Station was built on Walnut Street in the late 1950s.

Gadsden's Fire Department takes time out of a busy schedule to pose for this pre–World War II photograph. From left to right are the following: (standing) L.J. Scott, W.B. Campbell, J.C. Bellamy, Hugh McManama, Gene Roberson, J.G. Hart, Jim Brooks, Lanice Glenn, Z.E. Wright, W.T. Cox, Allen Miller, Homer Holland, Bert Moss, "Cuzz" Hudson, Lee Helton, Homer O'Dell, Elbert Mount, Clyde Landers, and Sol Green; (on ladder truck) Tillerman and Winkleman; (on other firetrucks) Roddy Sutton, Horace Hale, H.G. Parnell, F.M. Morgan, L. Stokes, E.D. Gross, Napoleon Wigginton, Arnold Johnson, Fred Helton, Jimmy Miller, DeWitt Robison, and W.H. Bobo.

Members of the first fire medic program are shown in a photograph from early 1973. An old fire engine was repainted and reoutfitted to become Rescue One. Shown are Jerry Fuller, Ted Moring, Rick Stallo, B.D. Payne, Clark Kennedy, Travis Johnson, Jim Garrard, Mike Thornton, and Jim Turner, standing in front of the "White Goose".

The gates to Camp Sibert are busy as shown in this photograph taken in 1944. The giant military installation was a chemical warfare training facility which covered a large area of Etowah County during the war years. The camp also housed a POW camp during the later days of the war. The installation was phased out at the close of the war. Little remains in this area today that would indicate the camp was even here.

A P-40 fighter plane is flying high over Etowah County's Camp Sibert during World War II. The planes, including P-39s, A-24 dive bombers, A-25 torpedo bombers, and A-20 and B-25 medium-range bombers, were used to train pilots at the camp. The camp's runway is located in the background in this photograph from 1944. The airport was deeded to the City following the end of the war. Camp Sibert was a chemical weapons training facility and also contained a prisoner-of-war camp. The chemical weapons training facility was moved to Ft. McClellan in Anniston when Camp Sibert was closed, following the end of WW II.

A "tent city" was used as temporary housing at Camp Sibert during World War II. The camp was home for many soldiers during the years of the war and contributed much to the local economy of Attalla and Etowah County. Camp Sibert closed shortly after the war, and very little remains to remind local residents of this once important military installation.

A "birds-eye" view of Camp Cherokee is shown here in 1934. The Civil Conservation Corp. #444 was located in Glencoe and did work throughout Etowah County during the Great Depression. Captain William P. Brandon was the commander of the camp during its days in this area. The camp later moved from this area and relocated to Mississippi.

This is one of Gadsden's early steam fire engines in front of the original City Hall building. City Hall was located on North Fifth Street near Broad Street. The fire engine was drawn by a matched team of horses. Gadsden's Central Fire Station was also located in City Hall.

This is the present site of Gadsden's City Hall and Police Building. The complex was built on the banks of the Coosa River in 1960. City Hall is the building in the background, and the police building and the municipal court building are in the foreground. City Hall is located on the corner of First and Chestnut Streets.

This is one of the early photographs of Gadsden's Municipal Auditorium. Convention Hall, as it is called today, is the center for many big events in Etowah County. The auditorium has been extensively remodeled and attracts many shows and conventions to the Etowah County area today. The auditorium is shown here in a 1945 photograph.

This 1940 photograph shows the chapel located at Forrest Cemetery in Gadsden. This beautiful chapel is unique in its design and has sandstone shingles on its roof. Forrest Cemetery is one of the largest in Gadsden, and many of her prominent citizens have been laid to rest here.

This photograph shows Gadsden's Amphitheater across from the Municipal Auditorium. The amphitheater has been the scene of many band concerts, singings, and live shows throughout its many years of operation. A ring was set up on stage for a wrestling match in the 1950s. The amphitheater was named in memory of Dr. Mort Glosser in 1997. Dr. Glosser was Gadsden's superintendent of education for many years.

The Etowah County Commission is shown here in a 1935 photograph. From left to right are the following: Mark Smith (District Two), Will Smith (District One), W.F. Jeffers (commission chairman), Bill Chumley (District Three), and Milton Durham (District Four).

This is the old Etowah County Farm in 1948. This building also was the early home of McGuffey's Nursing home. Known in its early days as the "poor farm," people could go here that were homeless or without work. The County Farm was located on Highway 278 in Hokes Bluff.

This is Gadsden's beautiful Carnegie Library. The library was on the corner of Seventh Street and Broad Street, across from the First Baptist Church. The library, like many others throughout the country, was built with a $10,000 gift from Andrew Carnegie.

This is the interior of the children's department of the Gadsden Public Library, located on the corner of Seventh Street and Broad Street. The library, shown here in a 1938 photograph, was later moved to a larger and more modern structure on College Street.

This 1950s photograph shows the addition to the front of the Carnegie Library. This was Gadsden's first public library building. To the left of the library is the bus station, which was in operation in the downtown area for many years.

Attalla's beautiful post office is shown here under construction in 1935. The post office is located in downtown Attalla, near the railroads and the main business district. The post office has been in continuous operation since its completion.

This is one of the city of Attalla's early fire engines. This photograph from the early 1950s shows a truck with a front-end pump. Trucks such as this one were popular to use fighting grass fires. The Attalla Fire Department started out as a volunteer department in its early days, although today it is one of the most modern in north Alabama.

Members of the Attalla City Council take time out during one of their meetings to pose for a photograph. Shown from left to right are the following: Elmus Handy, Tom Wood, R.M. Cash, Mayor Charles Burke, Justin McClendon, M.L. Walker, and J. Ralph Brown. This photograph was taken during Charles Burke's term as mayor, which spanned the years 1940–1968.

Six

SCHOOLS

Walnut Grove, located in Western Etowah County during the late 1890s, was the home of the Grove Academy. This college was one of the leading schools in northeast Alabama until 1899. The academy offered a full curriculum and was well known for the high quality of its graduates.

Gadsden's first public school building was built in 1880 and was known as the Gadsden Public Institute. This school was attended by both boys and girls and was built on the present-day site of the Gadsden Public Library on College Street. The name was changed in 1881 to the Gadsden Female Institute. In later years, it was also known as the Chestnut Street School and the Central School.

Disque High School was Gadsden's first public high school. The brick school was built in 1901 at the present site of the Gadsden Post Office. This structure served as a high school until 1924, at which time Gadsden High School opened. Disque Junior High School was here from 1924 until 1941. This building later housed the Gadsden Board of Education. This was the first brick school building in the Gadsden area.

This is a class at McCauley's Chapel Methodist Church in 1917. The people pictured here include the following: Carl Reece, Sherman Stovall, Bailey, Clyde Reece, Britt Reece, Winnie David Bullard, Lurenda Nipper Cox, Becky Findley, Mrs. Reece, Tom Hanson, Oscar Henson, Emma Lankford Stovall, Bertha Davis Marona, Gertie Sitz Sherrill, Thelma Lanford Griffin, Myrtly Reece, Vera Davis Spurgeon, Lillian McBrayer, Odis Nipper, Ben Davis, Leslie Davis, Gussie Davis, and Edgar Sitz.

This was one of Gadsden's early elementary schools. The Eleventh Street School was erected in 1907 at a cost of $18,000. This brick structure was the second brick building built by the Gadsden Board of Education. The school later closed when newer schools were built in this area. The aging structure was later renovated and now houses the Gadsden Board of Education.

The Victory Hill School was a classic example of the small country schoolhouse in the Etowah County area. This small school was located just south of Attalla in rural Etowah County. Schoolhouses such as this one have long since given way to large, modern brick county schools.

This was the original building of the John Jones School in Rainbow City, one of the early schools in the Rainbow City area. The school has grown and is now in an ultra-modern structure and is a fine example of Etowah County's attempts to offer the finest in education.

Glencoe was one of the earlier county schools in the Etowah County system. The school was built in 1918. Only Disque High School in Gadsden and Etowah High School in Attalla are older. The school was a two-story, white frame building. The first graduate of Glencoe High School was David Gray.

Four young students from Southside School are shown here in front of the buildings. From left to right are Joe Pat Slay, J.L. Fuhrman, Ed Roy Routon, and Bobby Vinson. The school was opened in 1927. A modern brick school was later built to replace this aging structure.

Pilgrims Rest School was located near Southside. This was a fine example of the small schools found in the different communities throughout Etowah County. The small schoolhouses that were once the center of learning in our county have now been replaced with the finest education has to offer.

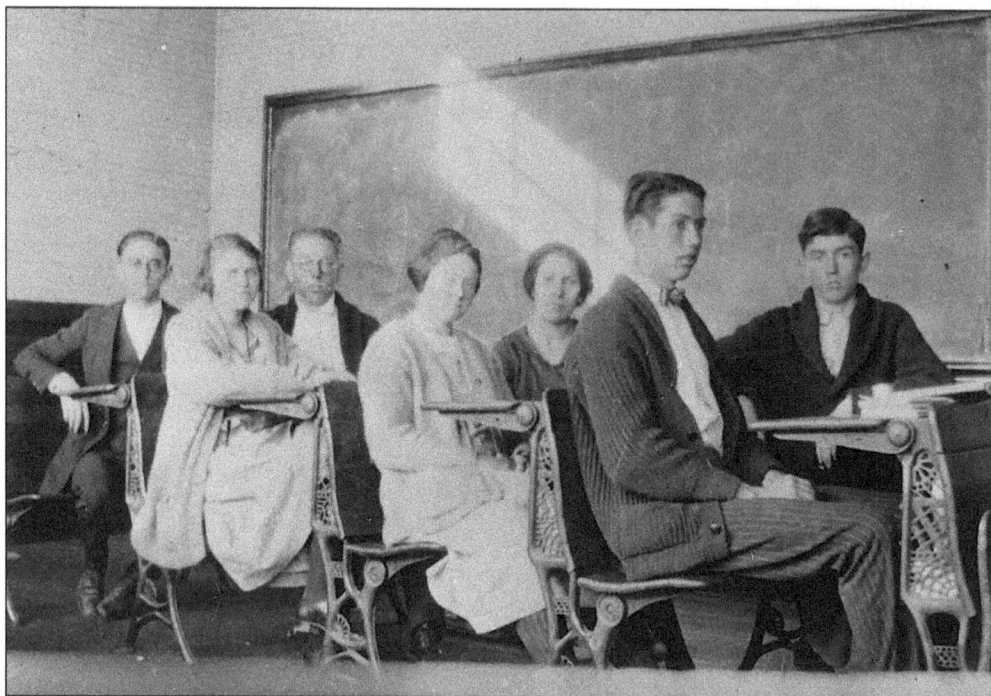

Students are seen here attending a class at Walnut Grove High School in 1926. This classroom, like so many others in the early Etowah County Schools, was small and sometimes crowded. The schools were small, wood-frame buildings, and the rooms were usually heated with a large pot-bellied stove.

The first Dwight Elementary School was located on Peachtree Street in Alabama City. This early-1900 photograph shows the original school built in the mill village. The company provided schools, a bowling alley, a bandstand, a ball park, and a large lake complete with a bathhouse for their employees.

This is Gaston High School as it looked in 1940. The school is located just north of Gadsden on Highway 411. The school was built in 1920 and was one of the early Etowah County public schools. The wood-frame structure was destroyed in a fire in 1959. A modern brick structure now houses Gaston High School.

This is one of the many classrooms in the original Gaston High School building. This classroom, like many others in the early schools, was small and conditions were crowded. A single pot-bellied stove in the corner was used to heat the classrooms on cold winter mornings.

This was the original building of the Etowah County High School, located in Attalla, Alabama. This school was the earliest high school in the Etowah County School system. The Etowah "Blue Devils" have had outstanding athletic programs dating back to the early 1900s. Etowah High School is located in a modern school building and is now part of the Attalla School system.

This 1929 Chevrolet, four-cylinder bus was one of Etowah County's first school buses in 1929. This bus transported students from the Tabor community to Etowah County High School. The students could walk up the mountain faster than the bus would pull it. They are, from left to right, as follows: (inside the bus) Francis Reeves, Gladys Winningham, Ruth Means, Mary Morgan, Ruby Lee Hill, Daisy Blackwell, Doris Walden, Irene Ellen, and Margaret Riddle; (outside of bus) Verdia Adams, Eddie Dangler, Mable Murphy, William Murphy, Chambers, Wilson Logan, Anderson Morgan, and Marion Smith, driver.

This was the Altoona High School Marching Band in 1941. Altoona High School was located in western Etowah County, near the Blount County line. Peter Roberts was the band director. Altoona High School and Walnut Grove High later merged to form West End High School. Although Altoona High was one of the smaller schools in Etowah County, it had an outstanding high school band.

Gulfsteel Junior High School was built in Alabama City in 1936. The school contained 16 classrooms, a lunchroom, and 6 other rooms. The school building was later enlarged and became the Emma Sansom High School. This structure was later torn down, and a new high school building was erected on this site.

Located atop the mountain across from Noccalula Falls is the R.A. Mitchell Elementary School. This school was built in 1948 on land donated by Mrs. Sadie Elsmore. The school was renamed in memory of Colonel Reuben A. Mitchell, a former mayor of Gadsden. The school is still in operation as one of Gadsden's fine elementary schools.

104

A second grade class from Oak Park Elementary School is shown in this photograph. The class was taught by Mrs. D.A. Vann. Oak Park School was erected in 1923 near the main entrance to the Republic Steel Corporation. It became a part of the Gadsden School System when Alabama City and Gadsden merged in 1932. The school is no longer in existence.

Gadsden High School is shown here in a photograph from the late 1940s. The school, located on North Twelfth Street, had been in use 20 years when this photo was taken. Only a handful of cars can be seen parked in the horseshoe-shaped driveway. Very few students or teachers had cars following World War II.

The gutted remains of Gadsden High School are shown here still smoldering following a destructive fire in November of 1972. The main building and auditorium were gutted and had to be rebuilt. Students attended classes in the remaining buildings on a split schedule the balance of the school year. Although the following school year started six weeks late, the Class of 1974 graduated from a newly renovated school building.

Pictured here are members of the South Eleventh Street School Rhythm Band. Music, as well as art, was an important part of the course of study in the grammar schools throughout Gadsden. This photograph was taken during the school year of 1937.

St. James Catholic Church operates a large private school in the Gadsden area. The school was located near the church in this early photograph of the original school building. The school, which provided kindergarten through the eighth grade, is now located in the North Gadsden area.

Built in 1926, the Elliott Grammar School was named in memory of Captain James M. Elliott, one of the founders of Alabama City. The building was remodeled in 1950. The grammar school was located on Elliott Avenue, which is now known as Meighan Boulevard. When several schools were consolidated, this facility was renovated and became the Elliott Community Center.

107

This was Gadsden's Carver High School in 1963, located on Tuscaloosa Avenue. The school was known for its outstanding athletic programs and had one of the finest high school bands around. The school was closed in the early 1970s and much of the building was torn down. The gymnasium now houses a recreation center. This school will long be remembered for its outstanding curriculum and notable educators.

This is a seventh grade class from Gulf Steel Junior High School. Students shown in the photograph include the following: Eloise Rhinehart, Bonnie Burns, Elaine Woodward, Bennie Lou O'Brien, Barbara Entrekin, Dorcas Jones, Vera Nell Dobbs, Betty Stanfield, Mary Ruth Smith, Dolores Rickles, Louise Huddleston, Jean Rice, Ann Williams, Gaynell Battles, Doris Ann Brittain, Betty Nell Cryar, Sybil Jones, Frankie Nix, Joyce Lipscomb, Blonnie Haymes, Geraldine Stewart, Marjorie Ruth Jones, Jeanette Fulmer, Mary Frances Jordon, Doris June Gray, Christian Nash, Doris Jewell Duke, Myra Blevins, Lucy Elmore, Beatrice Crow, and Betty Rose Hopkins. Gulf Steel Junior High is now the site of Emma Sansom High School. The middle school is presently named General Forrest Middle School.

108

Seven

Transportation

Captain William M. Elliott is shown here in the center of one of the locks on the Coosa River. Many riverboats were used to transport a variety of freight on the river. The Coosa River was the main route of trade before the coming of the railroads to this area in the late 1800s.

Larger streetcar rails are being installed in the Gadsden and Attalla area in this 1912 photograph. The streetcars ran throughout Gadsden, Alabama City, and Attalla until 1934. A large labor force was needed to change the miles and miles of rails.

A large group of passengers are shown preparing to board one of the many streetcars which operated between Attalla and Gadsden in this 1915 photograph. The streetcar line ran between the railroad terminal in Attalla and downtown Gadsden. A line also ran up the mountain to Noccalula Falls, a popular tourist attraction.

Two riverboats are shown near the Alabama Furnace Company in this 1916 photograph. The riverboat at the right was converted and used as a dredge on the Coosa River near Gadsden. There were, at one time, over 30 riverboats operating on the Coosa River between Rome, Georgia, Gadsden, and Greensport, Alabama.

One of the many Louisville and Nashville trains that operated throughout the Etowah County area is shown here in this photograph from 1905. The crew of Engine 800 shown here are, from left to right, as follows: engineer L.B. Curry, brakeman Earl Williams, switchman Bud Yoe, and fireman Arthur Hughes. The railroads have contributed much to the economy of Etowah County during the twentieth century.

The Coosa River is seen here above flood stage in a 1916 Lebourg photograph. The city wharf is shown here almost totally submerged in the waters of the river. The Emma Sansom Monument is seen in the center of the photograph. This is the present site of the Memorial Bridge in Gadsden.

This early Adolph Lebourg photograph from 1917 shows Hokes Bluff road long before it was paved and became Hoke Street. This was an important thoroughfare between Gadsden and the Hokes Bluff area of Etowah County. This road was heavily traveled until the Highway 278 cutoff was built between the two towns.

This is one of the many streetcars that ran from Attalla through Alabama City and on to Gadsden. The Alabama City, Gadsden, and Attalla Railroad Company was owned by Captain J.M. Elliott Jr. during its years of operation. The streetcar service was discontinued in 1934 when bus service came into operation in the Etowah County area.

A Louisville and Nashville (L & N) train is shown crossing the Coosa River in this 1918 photograph. The gasoline-powered riverboat, the *Captain Lyerly*, built in 1913, is also shown at the wharf in Gadsden. The L & N trestle was the first bridge built across the river in this area and was also used for automobile and pedestrian traffic.

113

This *c.* 1910 photograph shows Dr. M.P. Hughes in one of the early automobiles in the Etowah County area. Dr. Hughes was one of the early physicians in Gadsden and helped to build some of the buildings in the downtown area. The automobile shown is a two-cylinder Maxwell.

Canterberry Station was a major part of Alabama City's business district. Grocery stores, feed stores, millinery shops, drugstores, and movie theaters were all located here. The streetcar from Gadsden to Attalla stopped here to pick up students who attended Disque or Etowah High Schools. Talmadge and Hiram Thacker are shown here in front of Alabama City Livery. Note the four-digit phone number.

The Keener Depot is shown here in an early-1900 photograph. Keener is located near Attalla and was on the railroad route from Chattanooga to Birmingham. Keener was a mining community located near the Etowah-Dekalb County lines.

Dave Underwood is standing beside a truck from Gadsden Steam Laundry. The truck was an electric truck and its batteries had to be recharged overnight. This photo is an early-1920s photograph showing one of Gadsden's early downtown businesses. Please note the early two-digit phone number on the truck's side.

Mr. and Mrs. Ed W. Robertson and family are shown in this 1909 photograph. The photo was made on Broad Street, in front of the present site of the Choice Restaurant. The vacant lot in the background is the present site of the Snellgrove Building with the Federal Courthouse to the right. Also pictured are, from left to right, the following people: Pauline (Mrs. Marvin H.) Brown, son James F. Robertson, daughter Rosella (Mrs. Byron) Gilliland, the daughter of Othamay (Mrs. Roy) Vann, and housekeeper Miss Florence Dismukes.

Gilbert's Ferry was one of the many ferries operating on the Coosa River throughout the Etowah County area. This ferry was located at Southside, at the present site of the Mark Smith Bridge. The ferry was in operation until this bridge was completed. This 1920 photograph shows Mrs. Adolph Lebourg seated in the wagon crossing the river.

116

The Lowe and James Motor Express hauled freight in the Birmingham, Gadsden, and Atlanta areas. Freight carriers such as these were important to large industry in the Etowah County area. Improved highways and diesel trucks brought the era of riverboat trade in the area to a close.

This 1907 photograph shows the *City of Gadsden* near the Gadsden Wharf on the Coosa River. Captain D.H. Johnson is standing on the cotton bale. The riverboats were important to commerce in the Gadsden to Rome trade routes. Hundreds of bales of cotton were shipped between the two cities each year. The home of Ike Lafollette, a noted riverboat captain, is in the background.

This 1940 photograph shows a railcar from the Tennessee, Alabama, and Georgia (TAG) Railroad. Cars such as this one were used to carry mail from Gadsden to Chattanooga, Tennessee. The TAG route ran through Etowah County and came into Gadsden from the north near Tuscaloosa Avenue. This railcar was known as the "Scooter."

Terminal Station, located on First Avenue, is shown here in this 1945 photograph. During the early years of the twentieth century, passenger train service was offered to the Gadsden area. The station was torn down shortly after train service was discontinued to this area, and this beautiful landmark was destroyed.

The Wagnon Ferry was one of several ferries operating on the Coosa River in the Etowah County area. Ferries such as this one were located in high-traffic areas before the bridges were built across the river. This ferry was in operation in 1959. The only ferry operating in the Etowah County area today is the Hokes Bluff Ferry.

This was a classic confrontation between an early automobile and a tree. Adolph Lebourg was fascinated by automobiles, motorcycles, and airplanes, and the contents of his work reflected this love. Many of Lebourg's photographs made throughout Etowah County were also people oriented.

A wagon loaded with baskets is shown in an early-1900s photograph. This photo was taken in front of the Etowah County Courthouse. The streetcar tracks are visible, and Broad Street is shown in an unpaved condition. This was also before additions and improvements were made to the courthouse.

Here, a Louisville and Nashville passenger train is crossing the railroad trestle heading for East Gadsden. Locomotive service was important to the Etowah County area during its early days, transporting both goods and passengers. The L & N trestle was the first bridge spanning the Coosa River in the Gadsden area. The trestle remains today much as it has for the past 100-plus years.

During the 1920s, airplanes would land and take off from a large field in East Gadsden adjacent to the Coosa River. These were the days before Etowah County had an airport. This early airfield was located at the present site of K-Mart. This photograph was taken by Adolph Lebourg.

An early Southern Airways plane is shown in front of the hanger at the Gadsden Airport. This hangar was destroyed in a fire in the early 1970s. Southern Airways offered flights from Gadsden to Atlanta on a daily basis. The Gadsden Airport was once a part of Camp Sibert during World War II.

Many people traveling to the Gadsden area would pass through the Gadsden Municipal Airport's modern terminal. At one time, air service was offered between Gadsden and Atlanta on a daily basis. Service was slowly cut back and eventually discontinued. Today there is currently no commercial air service to the Etowah County area.

Eight

PEOPLE

Emma Sansom, a 16-year-old Alabama City resident, will long be remembered for her act of bravery on a spring morning in 1863. The Union army, led by Abel Streight, was en route to Rome, Georgia, to capture the city. Approaching Gadsden, Streight burned the bridge across Black Creek near the Sansom home. Confederate General Nathan Bedford Forrest arrived shortly thereafter and found the bridge in flames. Emma Sansom offered to show the pursuing Confederates a ford which was used for cattle upstream from the bridge. Sansom mounted the general's horse and began to lead the Confederates up the creek. Gunfire from Union snipers broke out, with a bullet going through Miss Sansom's skirt. Forrest immediately stopped and had Sansom mount the horse behind him. He said that he would not be found in history to have hidden behind the skirt of a girl. Confederate cavalryman Robert Turner was killed and was buried in the Sansom family cemetery. Forrest continued his pursuit, overtook the Union troops near Cedar Bluff, Alabama, and forced Streight to surrender. Forrest returned to the area a few days later to thank Miss Sansom for her daring act of bravery. The memory of this event was commemorated by the naming of Alabama City's high school—Emma Sansom High School.

The Confederate veterans are shown here in a reunion photograph at the Emma Sansom Monument. The monument is located near the Coosa River in downtown Gadsden. The Memorial Bridge was built near the statue and covered some of its base. This photograph, made in 1911, shows a large group of surviving veterans. Colonel R.B. Kyle, Gadsden's first mayor, is seated at the far left.

In 1919, B. Frank O'Bryant designed and built this small steam locomotive. The engine and coal tender was 16 feet long, 4 feet wide, and weighed 2,250 pounds. The construction took a total of 17 months. The locomotive was operated in an amusement park in Gadsden for several years by O'Bryant and William Young.

General William Luther Sibert is shown standing atop one of the locks of the Panama Canal. Sibert, known as "Goliath," was a native of Etowah County and a graduate of the United States Military Academy. Sibert was instrumental in the construction of the Gatum locks in the Panama Canal. Camp Sibert, a chemical warfare training center located near Gadsden, was named in memory of him.

Fordy Edwin Reed is shown standing by a McClain Dairy Truck from this 1949 photograph. McClain's Dairy Farm was located at Stowers Hill in Attalla. The truck advertised pasteurized milk, which had just come on the market at this time.

Hazel Brannon Smith was a 1930 graduate of Gadsden High School. Her career began as a newspaper publisher late in the 1930s. She had a prosperous and successful life as a newspaper owner in the state of Mississippi. Her life was marked by glorious highs that included a Pulitzer Prize in 1964 that brought her national fame.

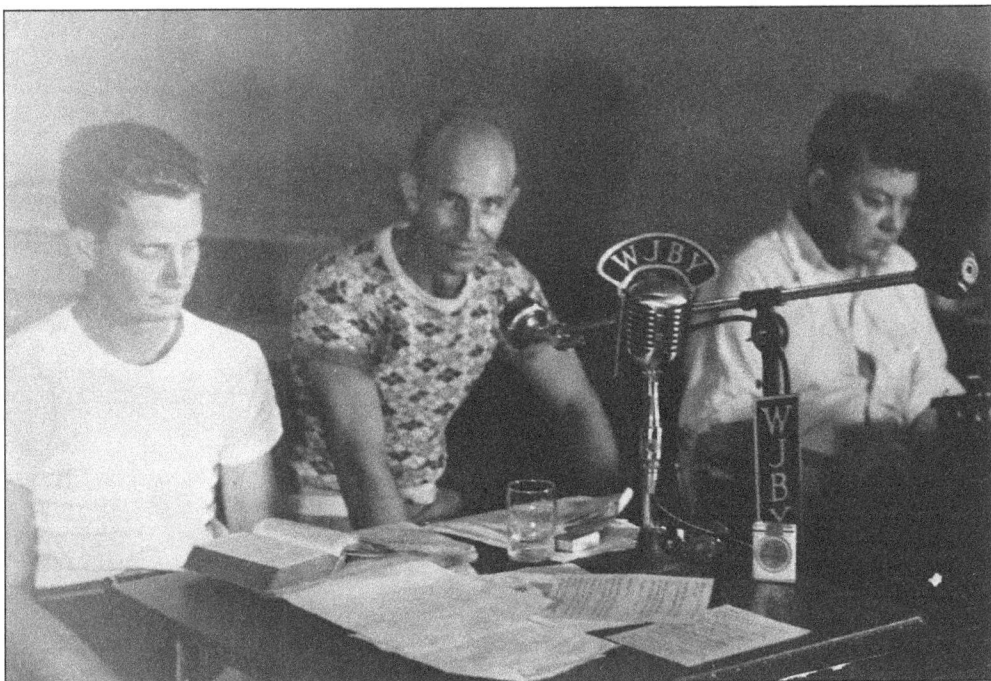

WJBY radio was one of Gadsden's early radio stations. The photograph from early 1941 shows, from left to right, Ray Cox, Larry Brunes, and Jack Kirby. Radio was important to the residents of Etowah County during this time period before the days of television. WJBY is still on the air in the Etowah County area.

Kitty and Smiley Wilson were local hometown folks. They were radio personalities and appeared on WGAD's Dixie Jamboree held at the Gadsden City Auditorium every Saturday night in 1954. They left Gadsden and became part of the Grand Ole Opry. They have a daughter who is also a recording artist known as "Little Rita Faye."

In 1944, Albert M. Rains was elected congressman from the Fifth Alabama District and filled that office with distinction until his retirement 20 years later. Rains was a prominent attorney practicing in the Gadsden area before his election to the House of Representatives, a position he held during the terms of five different presidents. Representative Rains sponsored many bills which provided housing for low-income families. Because of these efforts, he was known as "Mr. Housing–USA." He was also remembered as the silver-tongued orator for his eloquent speeches. Upon his retirement from Washington, Rains and his wife, Allison, returned home to the Gadsden area. A portion of Highway 411, which runs parallel to the Coosa River, was renamed "Albert Rains Boulevard" in honor of Representative Rains.

www.ingramcontent.com/pod-product-compliance
Lightning Source LLC
Chambersburg PA
CBHW080628110426
42813CB00006B/1633